AMAZING
AMSTERDAM

Andy Herbach
Karl Raaum

MADE EASY TRAVEL GUIDES
www.madeeasytravelguides.com
AMAZING AMSTERDAM
Andy Herbach and Karl Raaum
First edition © 2023
ISBN: 9798872688907
Photo credits and descriptions on pages 75 and 76.

TABLE OF CONTENTS

1. INTRODUCTION

Amsterdam has more canals than Venice, more bridges than Paris, more bicycles than cars, and perhaps more tolerance than any other city in the world. It's what makes Amsterdam truly unique and such a wonderful place to visit. Because the city is so compact, you can see a lot even if your stay is short. Its sights are as diverse as its residents, including beautiful churches, lovely gardens, world-class museums and, of course, the infamous Red-Light District. Cultured, vibrant, fun-and easy to get around-Amsterdam is the perfect European city to explore.

Heineken
meest getapt

Heineken
Het meest getapt ·

ineke

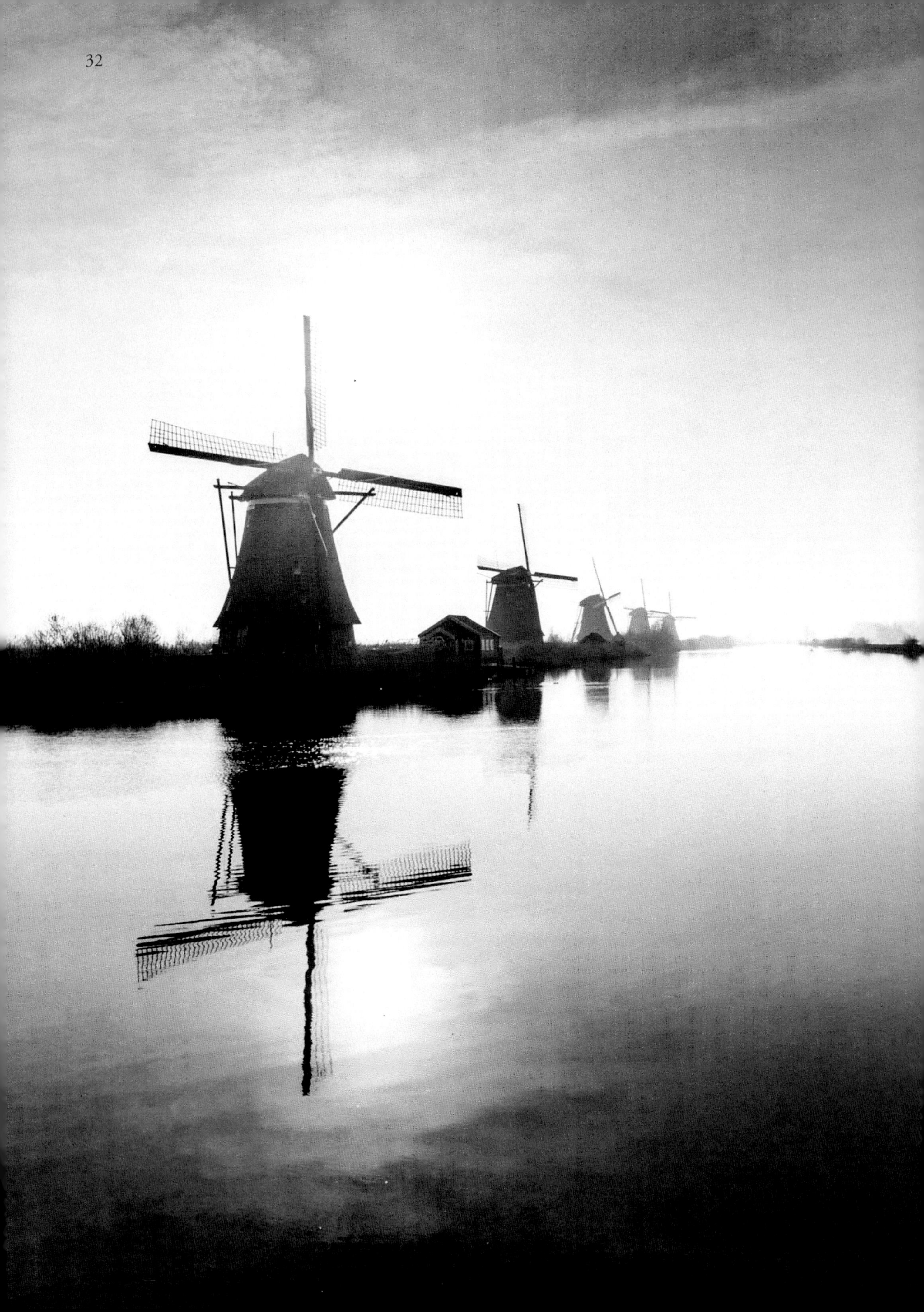

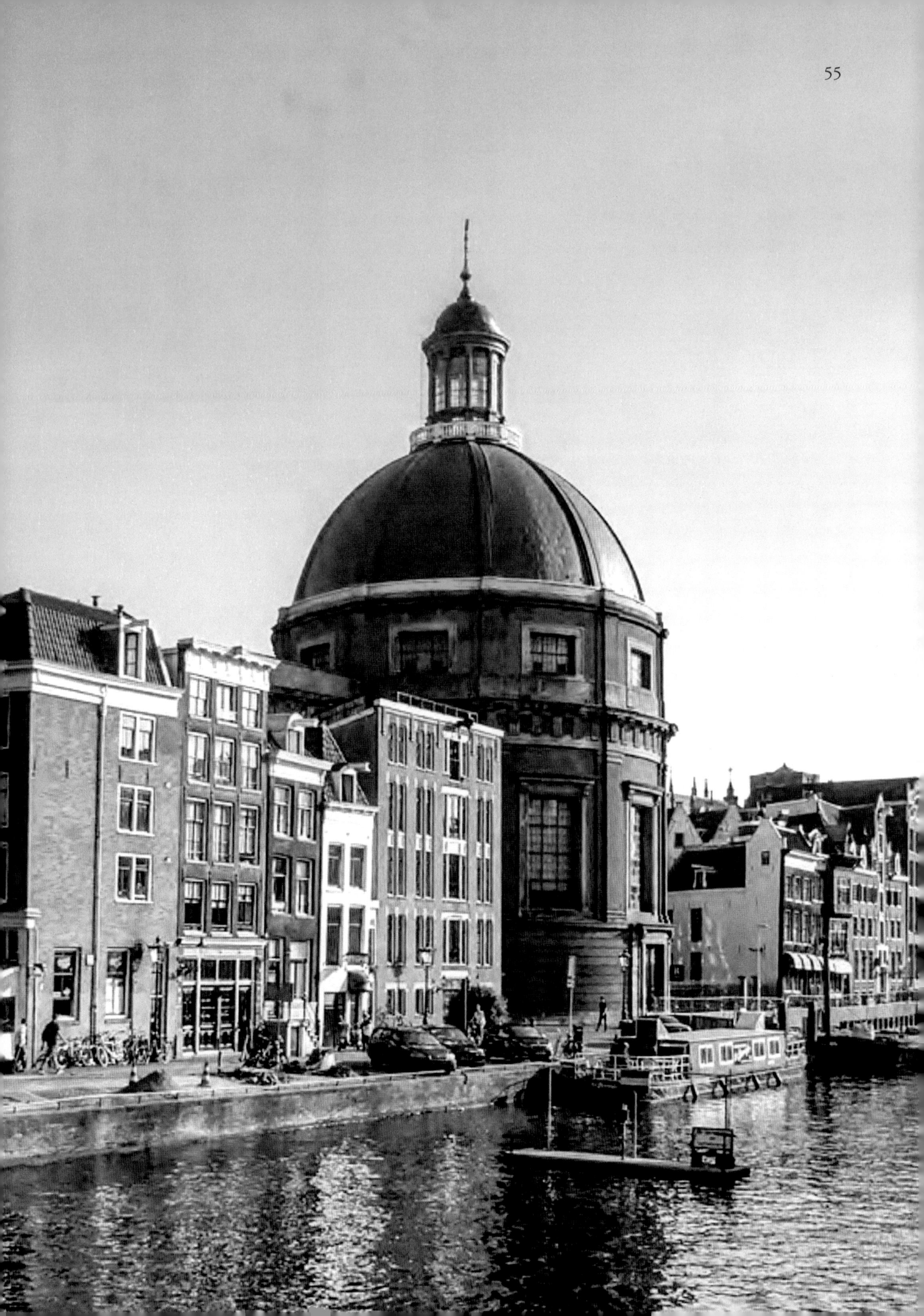

HET SCHEEPVAARTMUSEUM

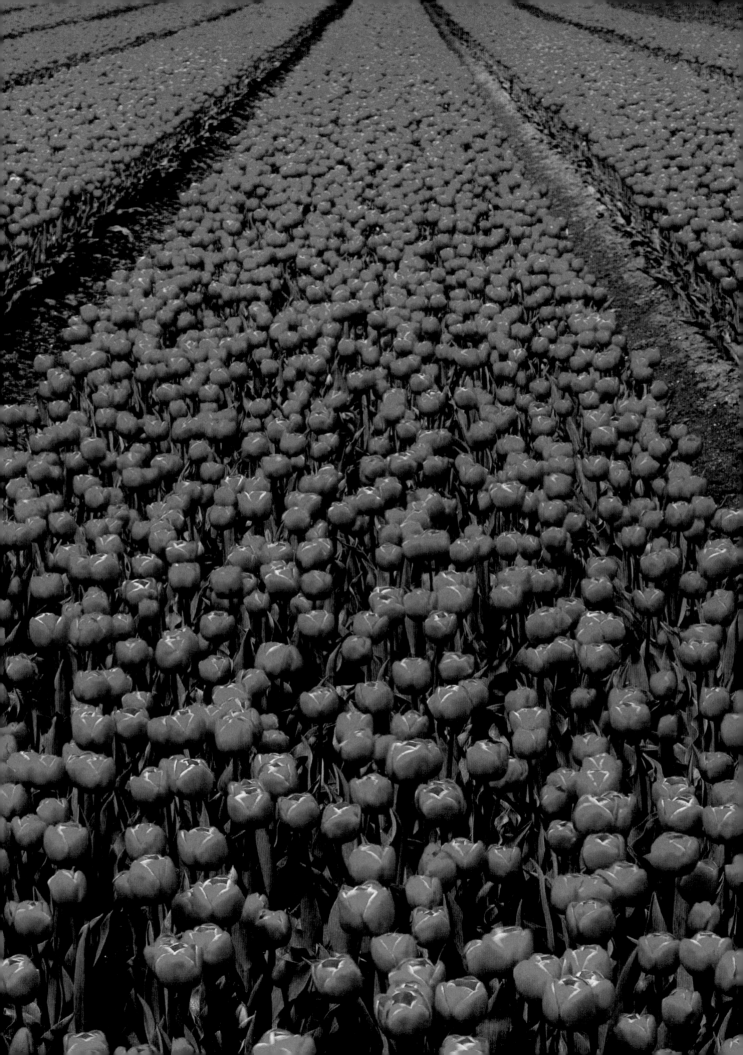

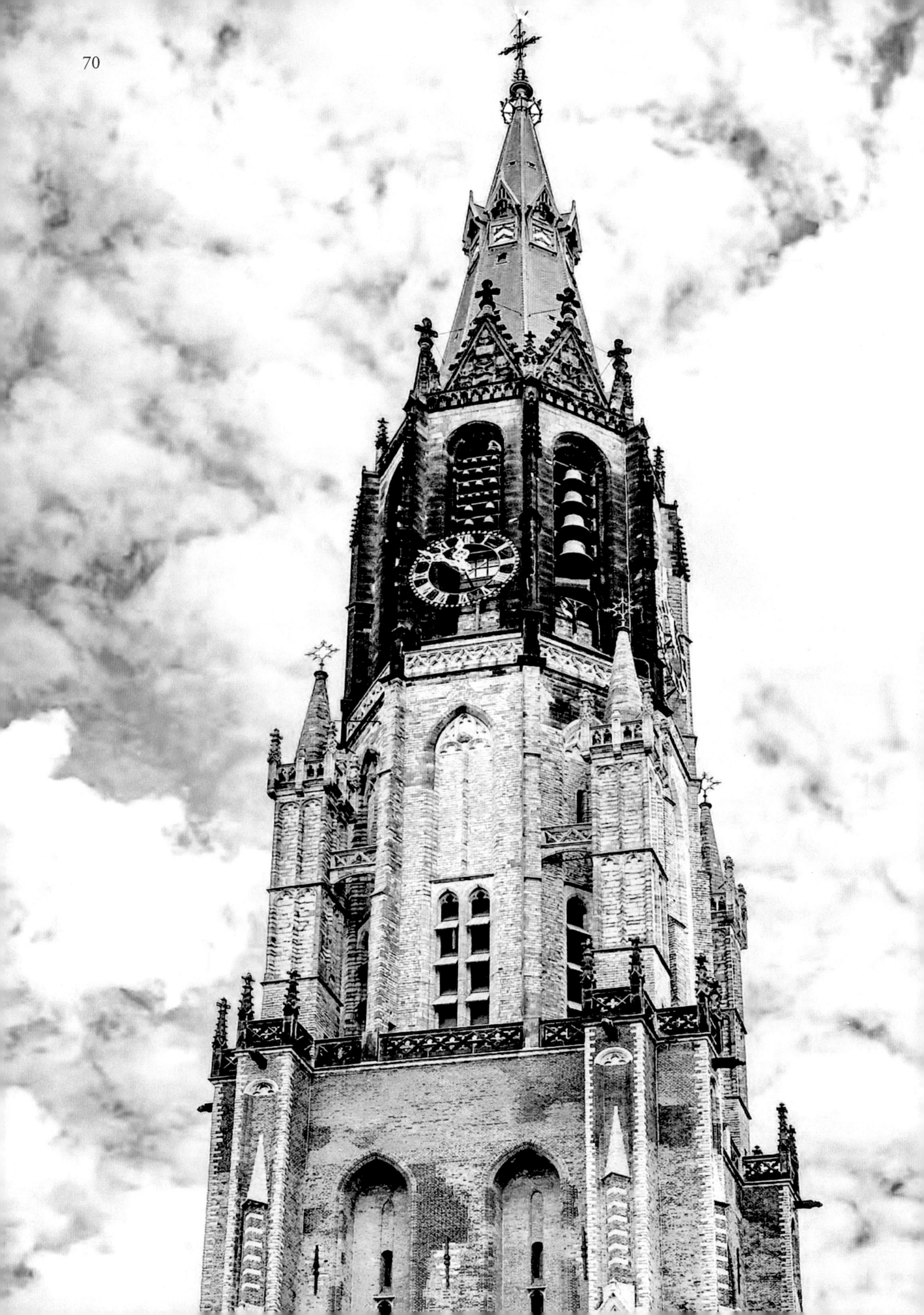

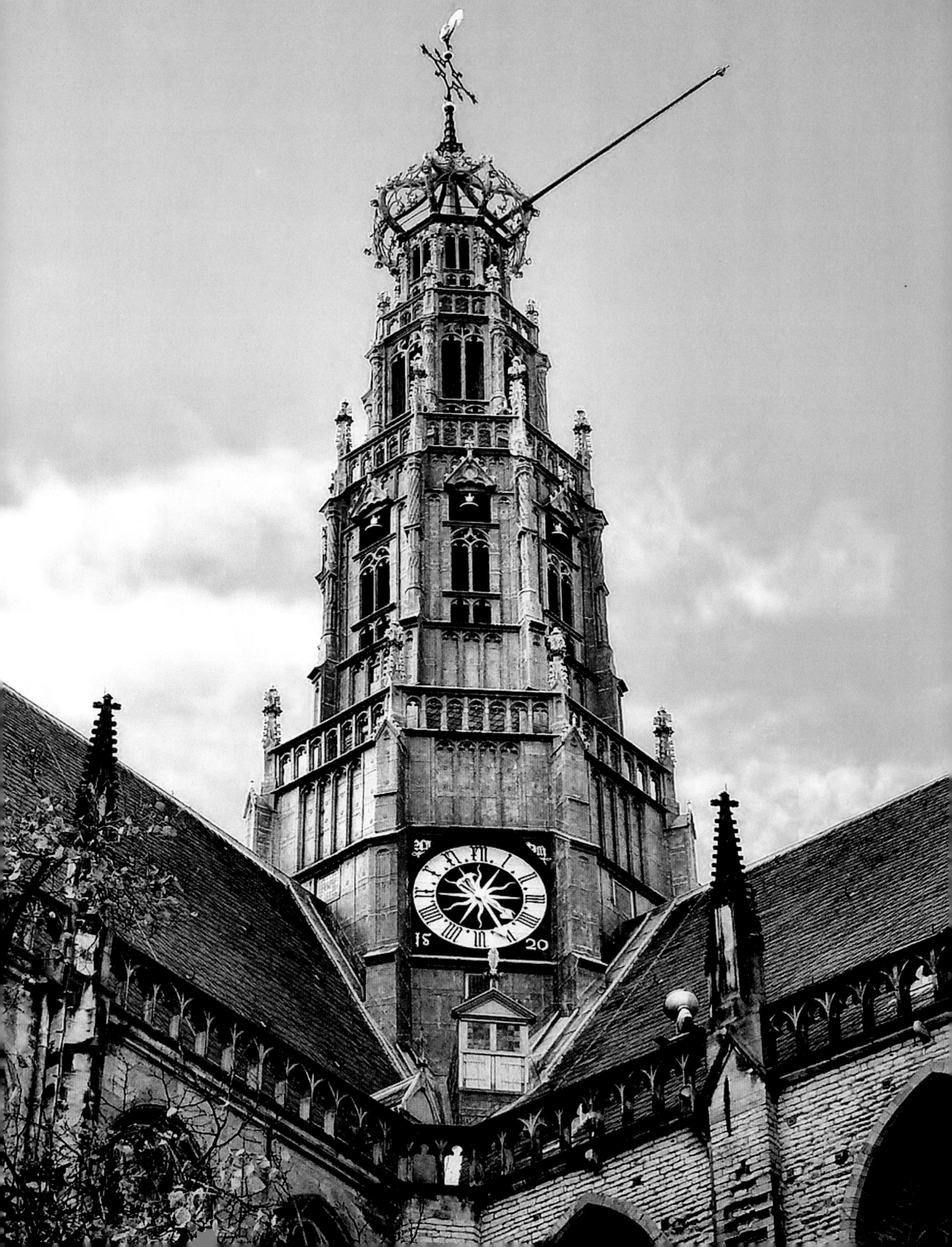
15 20

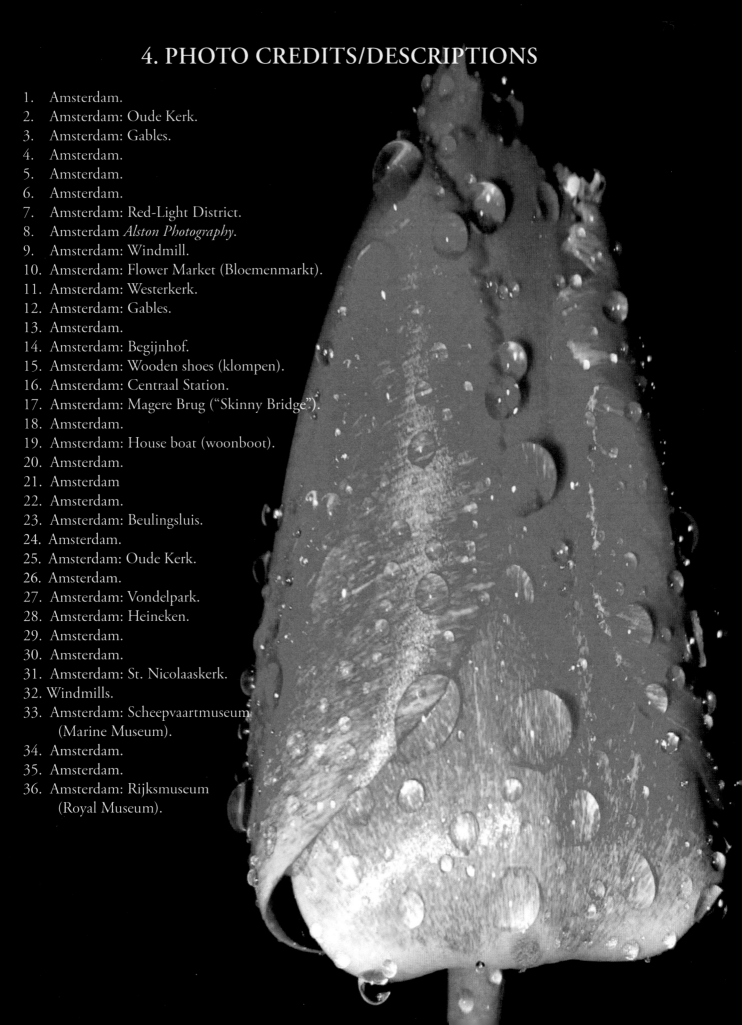

4. PHOTO CREDITS/DESCRIPTIONS

1. Amsterdam.
2. Amsterdam: Oude Kerk.
3. Amsterdam: Gables.
4. Amsterdam.
5. Amsterdam.
6. Amsterdam.
7. Amsterdam: Red-Light District.
8. Amsterdam *Alston Photography*.
9. Amsterdam: Windmill.
10. Amsterdam: Flower Market (Bloemenmarkt).
11. Amsterdam: Westerkerk.
12. Amsterdam: Gables.
13. Amsterdam.
14. Amsterdam: Begijnhof.
15. Amsterdam: Wooden shoes (klompen).
16. Amsterdam: Centraal Station.
17. Amsterdam: Magere Brug ("Skinny Bridge").
18. Amsterdam.
19. Amsterdam: House boat (woonboot).
20. Amsterdam.
21. Amsterdam
22. Amsterdam.
23. Amsterdam: Beulingsluis.
24. Amsterdam.
25. Amsterdam: Oude Kerk.
26. Amsterdam.
27. Amsterdam: Vondelpark.
28. Amsterdam: Heineken.
29. Amsterdam.
30. Amsterdam.
31. Amsterdam: St. Nicolaaskerk.
32. Windmills.
33. Amsterdam: Scheepvaartmuseum
    (Marine Museum).
34. Amsterdam.
35. Amsterdam.
36. Amsterdam: Rijksmuseum
    (Royal Museum).

All photos from Pixabay.com, except as noted.

This coffee table book features the photography found in the travel guide *Amsterdam Made Easy: Walks and Sights of Amsterdam.*

www.madeeasytravelguides.com

eed5007c-da23-43d8-b405-d9d7c37a97ffR01